WHITBY
A Pictorial History

An artist's impression of Whitby as it might have been in the days when the abbey was at the height of its power. The picture shows the magnificent monastery and the parish church, surrounded by a walled enclosure. Below can be seen the roofs of the tiny fishing village which developed into the present town.

WHITBY
A Pictorial History

Colin Waters

Phillimore

1992

Published by
PHILLIMORE & CO. LTD.
Shopwyke Hall, Chichester, Sussex

ISBN 0 85033 848 4

Printed and bound in Great Britain by
BIDDLES LTD.
Guildford, Surrey.

List of Illustrations

Frontispiece: Whitby Abbey prior to dissolution

Acknowledgements

Though the photographs in this book are drawn from the collection of the Whitby Pictorial Archives Trust, it would be unfair to assume that no acknowledgements are necessary. It is to the credit of Whitby people (and to others who live outside the town), that through their generosity in giving photographs to the Trust, Whitby Archives is able to preserve these images for future generations. My thanks are due to each and every one (many of them anonymous) who, like myself, share the belief that though valuable as private possessions, old photographs achieve a greater value when brought to a wider audience.

Photographs 69, 83 and 84 are by kind permission of Mr. Tom Roe, whose immense knowledge of jet, and the history of the town in general, is always freely given.

The map of Whitby's sea defences in 1794 (no. 61) was re-drawn from an original, by Mr. Eddie Newton.

Illustrations 7, 27, 48, 58, 71, 81, 108, 124, 132, 145, 149, 164, 165 and 169 are from the author's own collection.

Introduction

Few towns of its size in Britain can match the diversity of Whitby's historical connections or its impressive list of notable residents and visitors. Their deeds throughout the years have created an atmosphere which pervades every narrow street and alleyway of this quaint red-bricked town. In their wake they have left a legacy of historical worth and proud achievement which permeates all aspects of the town's community to this day.

There is little doubt that Whitby's first settlers were attracted to the area by its geographical position. The River Esk which separates the old and new areas of the modern town has long provided a natural haven for seafarers. It rises in a desolate moorland hollow at the head of Westerdale, and follows its meandering course through a number of picturesque villages, growing in size until it meets the town's natural harbour. Beyond the harbour entrance, Dunsley Bay (believed to be the Dunus Sinus mentioned by Ptolemy) itself forms a place of refuge for storm bound vessels, whilst the three miles of flat sands between Whitby and Sandsend provided a natural landing place for flat-bottomed vessels.

The fertile lands surrounding the river valley no doubt provided a means of survival for the inhabitants of the area long before recorded history, whilst its isolated position has meant that the wild moorland which surrounds the town for a good 20 miles in all directions has formed a natural barrier against landborne invasions, both friendly and hostile. Stone and bronze age man have left their calling cards in this region. A profusion of archaeological evidence has been found on sites across these rolling moorlands. Romans, Saxons, Vikings and Normans all helped shape the town, and remains of their existence are evident in the buildings and place names to be found throughout the region. The earliest documented inhabitants of the district were the Brigantes, who were in occupation at the time of the Roman invasions.

In early days the sea provided Whitby's only reliable means of access, and indeed it was by this method that the Romans first arrived in the area, setting up a string of signal stations and building the Roman road which is still to be seen on nearby Wheeldale moor.

The area's isolation would have made it an ideal situation for religious houses, and it would seem that a number of wattle and daub priories and abbeys may have existed here over the years. The first known monastery of Streonshalh (the ancient name for Whitby) was of the Order of Iona, and was founded in 658 by King Oswy of Mercia who appointed Hilda (or more accurately Hild, later to be known as St Hilda), Abbess of Hartlepool, as its first abbess. This was to fulfil a vow made following the defeat of Penda in battle. The monastery was established as a double house for both male and female adherents to the Celtic church and it became a great seat of learning, where many religious personages, including a number of bishops of York, were trained and educated.

The year 664 saw the Synod of Whitby, when bishops and other leaders of the Roman and Celtic churches gathered to decide the date for the celebration of Easter. Though Hilda was of the Celtic persuasion, King Oswy was inclined to the Roman beliefs which prevailed, resulting in a decision which was accepted throughout the Christian world and which governs the date of Easter to the present day.

Of the many great names which are associated with Whitby Abbey, that of Caedmon is perhaps the most legendary. Tradition tells us that Caedmon (the 'Father of English Poetry') was a young abbey cowherd who refused to join in the communal evening singing at the abbey. As he slept, whilst looking after cattle, an angel appeared bidding him to sing of the creation. His composition was later to be recognised as the first piece of English poetry. In reality Caedmon was perhaps older and less lowly than the legend would have us believe; it seems certain, however, that the story of the vision and his later life as a monk within the walls of the abbey are drawn from actual facts. Whatever the truth of Caedmon's origins, his fame lives on in Whitby, where a memorial cross has been erected in his honour at the top of the 199 steps.

Bede's History and the Anglo-Saxon Chronicle record the death of Hilda in the same year, 680, after which Hilda's pupil, the Princess Aelfleda, took over responsibility for the monastery at the age of 26, until her death in 713. In the year 867, following Viking raids on the community, the monks fled the town, and they may have taken the sacred relics of Hilda's bones with them.

It would seem that this was not the first occasion when Vikings had made their mark on the community, as the town's name at that time almost certainly had Scandinavian origins. It is known that the first records relating to Whitby refer to it by its earlier name of Streonshalh (also written as Streonschalr, Streanschalch, Streonshale etc., and pronounced Stren-shall). Historians have never agreed on the meaning of the name, or indeed that of Whitby itself, but it does at least seem possible that both names were brought by earlier settlers, who transferred the names of well-loved towns to their newly-founded settlements. Evidence to support this theory is not hard to find. A Norwegian trading port which lies close to Oslo carries the name of Skiringssalr which may be anglicised as Strineges-healle. The latter portion 'salr', or 'healle', directly translates as the English word 'hall'. Similarly the Scandinavian island of Gotland has as its capital the ancient walled town of Visby (formerly spelt Wisby), and in addition the island has a number of towns whose names bear close resemblance to villages in the countryside surrounding the town of Whitby.

It is also acknowledged by experts that Whitby's small fishing vessels known on this coast as cobles (pronounced cobbels), are based on the same design as traditional Viking longboats, and that the ancient street names such as Haggersgate, Baxtergate, Sandgate and Flowergate, and the short cobbled alleyways leading to the river, locally known as ghauts, derive directly from the old Norse word 'gata', which literally means 'street'; further proof, if it were needed, that Whitby owes much of its history to Scandinavian settlers.

Though originally intent on pillaging and looting, domestic Viking settlement of the area soon took place and a local seat of government, the Thingwalla, was established in the town.

For 207 years the history of the town and the abbey itself is not known, but in 1078 we find the Benedictine soldier-monk Reinfrid (who had formerly served with

William the Conqueror) in charge of rebuilding the (now Benedictine) monastery under the lord of the manor, William de Percy. It was de Percy who then held the manor under lease from Hugh, Earl of Chester, and who also granted land at Preistby for the support of Reinfrid. Though Preistby has never been positively identified, there is some evidence to show that it may well have been located at Fylingdales, in the Robin Hood's Bay area nearby.

It was at this time, in 1086, that Flowergate, one of Whitby's oldest thoroughfares, is mentioned, as it formed part of an ancient road by way of a ford across the river to the abbey. A bridge was not documented at this point until 1351.

In 1109 it is known that a leper hospital, founded by the monks of Whitby Abbey, was said to have been built (or rebuilt) at Spital Bridge (from which it takes its name). Its master at that time was Robert de Alnetto. It is interesting to note that this is one of the supposed sites of the first Whitby Abbey. Foundations from this hospital were still visible in 1816. The land at that time was owned by William Skinner and John Holt Junior who disturbed the remains and found three cellars of hewn flat stones. It was noted during exploration of these cellars that '... in them have been concealed two presses'. Just what kind of presses these were, or how long they had been concealed, was not recorded.

It was around this time that the parish church of St Mary was built, on the orders of William de Percy, for the residents of the town, as the abbey church was reserved for the monks and clergy. Modern visitors to the church are intrigued to find that its flat roof is constructed to represent the tween-decks of a ship, complete with hatch-like windows in the roof. This style of construction complements the high sided 17th-century box-like pews and the strange wooden balconies.

The original church, like the original abbey, was of wattle and daub. When it was first rebuilt in stone it had a higher tower than at present, a pitched roof, and a door which faced westward towards the harbour, all of which have now gone. The abbey itself continued to grow in size and importance over the years. Richard de Burgh built the eastern part including the choir in 1140, and perhaps followed this by constructing the chapter house, abbey church, lower tower and pillars. It was not until the late 1300s, however, that the upper part of the tower, the choir east wall and north transepts were completed. This was the work of the architect John of Brampton (Brompton). The remainder of the nave was constructed next, though this was finished in a more brown and less durable stone. The expansion of the abbey over the years was not without problems, both financial and otherwise. On a number of occasions work stopped due to insufficient funds, and on 10 November 1334 the newly completed south wall of the nave was blown down by one of the numerous gales which batter this exposed part of the north-east coast.

The 14th century saw the town of Whitby developing into a small trading port, and commerce and conflict with other parts of the country, including Scotland, were recorded. It is known that during this period lands near Kelso in Scotland were granted to Whitby Abbey, and numerous trading disputes occurred between the abbots and various individuals. A notation in the registers relating to disputes between Abbot Thomas de Malton and Alexander de Percy of Sneaton, around 1315, states that the Horngarth was constructed at Whitby with wood from the abbot's forest. Because of a complaint that Percy's men took more wood than was needed, selling the surplus in the town, it was later decided to deliver the wood direct to the abbot's office in order to prevent misappropriation of funds from the wood. It is possible that the Horngarth was a fenced area constructed annually to trap driven deer or cattle in order to de-horn them. Legend states that it was built as a penalty for the killing of a hermit monk who died whilst protecting a wild animal. It is said that if the hedge fails to stand three tides, then the lands of the lord of the manor shall be forfeited. The enclosure was always made up on Ascension Eve, unless the date happened to coincide with the feast of St John of Beverley. The Penny Hedge or Horngarth ceremony still takes place annually on Ascension Eve, in the Upper Harbour. Legend also links Robin Hood with this area. The outlaw is said to have stayed in the town as guest of the abbot, and the nearby village of Robin Hood's Bay was reputedly his hideaway during periods of refuge from the Sheriff of Nottingham.

It is known also that the trade in jet was being carried out at this time. Jet begins its life in seams in a similar way to coal, which it closely resembles. It is found only on the coastline around Whitby, and can be gathered from the seashore. Though its heyday was in the 1800s, mining began here long before, as jet beads and jewellery have been found in excavated prehistoric burial mounds from as far away as the Mediterranean. The abbey rolls list payments for jet rings as early as 1394, showing a continuous market through the years. During the days of Queen Elizabeth I, jet rosaries were common throughout the country.

By the 15th century the abbey residents and the people of the town, who had previously been virtually one community, began to live separately and in 1425 a proclamation by the king prevented the regular Sunday markets being held. It was perhaps at this time that the townspeople established their own market-place in the town, rather than in the vicinity of the market cross in the Abbey Plain, and market day was changed to Saturday.

One of the town's earliest real industries developed quickly with the discovery of alum rocks around Whitby in the year 1539. Though the abbey had now become a rich and powerful body, it was not to benefit from this new-found wealth, due to the dissolution of the monasteries the same year. Alum farming, as it was known, was carried out principally on what are now the lands of Lord Mulgrave at nearby Sandsend, where caves, tunnel entrances and bare hillsides still bear witness to the days of intense industry. The alum shale cliffs around Saltwick to the east have also been mutilated by the effects of mining, though the once substantial quays and piers which were constructed there have now long gone. Of all the trades and industries carried out in this area, it was perhaps alum more than any other which established Whitby as a shipping port, paving the way for the later days of shipbuilding and whaling.

The dissolution of the monasteries brought an end to the great period of learning which had given Whitby Abbey a reputation renowned throughout Europe. Under fiscal pressure and threat of an Act of Parliament, the abbot surrendered the abbey to the Crown Commissioners on 14 December 1539. Shortly afterwards the furniture and fittings were sold or otherwise disposed of, and the abbey gradually fell into disrepair. The monks were pensioned off or given grants of land, and between 1540 and 1555 the Cholmley family purchased the abbey lands, including 400 houses, 200 gardens, two watermills, one 'landmark', much agricultural land and all manorial privileges. Building materials from the structure of the abbey were used to build a manor, Abbey House, close by. The town was now free to develop in its own right, though in many ways it was still governed to a great extent by the whims of the new lord of the manor, who inherited immense power from his predecessor, the abbot.

The period that followed saw the town's involvement with a number of notable figures. Sir Richard Cholmley (the Great Black Knight of the North), Sir Thomas Fairfax and Peregrine Lascelles, all national historical characters of note, lived here in the days when the town was virtually cut off from the outside world except by sea. In later years other notables such as the pirate John Paul Jones, and the religious leaders George Fox (the Quaker) and John Wesley (the Methodist), all considered Whitby important enough to visit on a number of occasions.

The 17th century saw little change in the town. Despite the abbey's dissolution, the route across the river from east to west was still sufficiently important for a replacement bridge to be built in 1610. On a more serious note Browne Bushell, resident of Bagdale Hall, and a notorious turncoat who was a champion for both the Royalist and Parliamentarian causes, was executed on 29 March 1651. He had previously been in and out of custody on a number of political charges, including the handing over of Scarborough Castle to the Royalists in 1645, during the reign of Charles I. He was arrested at that time by his father-in-law, Sir Thomas Fairfax of Whitby. Despite involvement in political turmoil, it is pleasant to find that the business of the town went on as normal. No doubt light relief was experienced by the townsfolk in 1684, when the respected lord of the manor, Sir Hugh Cholmley, was fined three shillings, for failing to clean out 'Auder Waste'.

If the 1600s had seen the town's interests influenced by external events, then the 1700s reflected a more introspective phase of its development. In 1702 the rector of Sneaton, a known drunkard and rebel-rouser, was brought to court on a charge of attempting to procure local coble fishermen to transport his pregnant mistress out of the area, whilst in 1712 we are told of the farmers who would gather in the market to sell their wares each Saturday. The Old Market Place, as it is now known, is situated at the western end of Whitby bridge. It was here that Whitby's first post office was situated and where the stocks stood. In later years a building which housed the town's first printing press stood opposite the *Golden Lion* public house. The inn dates back to at least 1714, though it is thought that others may have been in existence here since the days when travellers to the abbey crossed the river at this point by ford or the bridge, which incidentally was replaced once more in 1766.

Whitby's first workhouse was constructed in 1727, indicating a large proportion of poor inhabitants, whilst 1757 saw a riot in the town when residents, mostly women, broke into and plundered the shops of meal sellers in protest at the corn monopoly.

The abbey by this time was becoming a crumbling ruin and in 1762 the south wall fell of its own accord. Whether this was due to structural decay, or whether the land in this area subsided, is not certain. What is sure is that the area directly below the abbey and parish church suffered a number of major landslips from this point onwards, often sending houses crashing down into the harbour, and leaving coffins from the graveyard above lying exposed to view.

The 18th century was perhaps the time of Whitby's greatest involvement with the sea. Captain James Cook, who learned his skills from ordinary Whitby sailors, put them to good effect during his charting of Canada's coastline, an achievement which later led to his voyage of discovery to Australia in 1769-70, using converted Whitby-built coal-carrying vessels. The same types of locally built vessels, known as cats, were also used for the voyage of the first fleet of settlers to that continent. During the years 1766 to 1816, whaling became a major industry and 2,761 whales were brought into the port. It was at this time also that the names of William Scoresby and his son, also

William, became famous. Scoresby senior was the inventor of the crow's nest and sailed further north than any other person, coming within just 500 miles of the pole. Scoresby junior acted as his ship's mate on that voyage. Whitby had now become a place of ships in which many ordinary families held part shares, and the town began to prosper.

Shareholding was not limited to shipping. In 1778 a new chapel dedicated to St Ninian was built, and paid for through shares held by local people. This house of worship is still owned today by shareholding individuals, its construction owing much to the skill of the shipbuilders of Whitby.

Smuggling was rife at this time, and in recent years a legendary smuggler's tunnel which formerly connected the old *Shiplaunch Inn* (now the Smuggler's Café) to the *Railway Tavern* (now the *Cutty Sark*) was rediscovered. Similarly, the nearby *Talbot Hotel* is known to have had a concealed 'stow-hold' beneath the floor of Talbot Cottage (now demolished) at its rear. Shareholding involved cash transactions and it was not long before the town's first bank was established in what for a number of years up to 1992 served as a pet shop on Whitby's east side. The fanlight above the door of the Church Street premises still shows the banker's name, J. Sanders.

Close to the shop stands the ancient *White Horse and Griffin Inn*. It was here in 1788 that Whitby's first diligence coach service began. Dickens was said to have stayed at the inn, which was renowned in its time as 'a haunt of gentlemen of certain standing'. Opposite the former banking premises stands the market-place, which was set up in 1640 to take over from what is now known as the Old Market Place on the far side of the bridge. The 'new' Toll Booth or Town Hall stands close by, having been designed and built in 1788 by the architect of the town piers and lighthouse, Jonathan Pickernell. The 'old' Toll Booth, which was built when the market-place was established by Sir Hugh Cholmley, itself replaced an earlier one further down Church Street.

By 1816, 2,761 whales were brought into the port with the addition of 2,500 seals, 55 bears, and 43 narwhals. Processing of the carcases was undertaken in order to provide gas for the lighting of the town, bones for women's corsets, and a whole range of other products; arches made from whales' jawbones were erected everywhere. Invention came from need and necessity, spawning many innovations, such as the swivel harpoon gun invented by a local man named Hall. His invention was presented to the Royal Society which awarded him a cash prize. With this money he purchased a mahogany grandfather clock, which played a different tune each day, and showed the position of the sun, moon, and tides. It would seem that the love of novelties was passed down through the generations, for his great grandson, Gibson Hall, owned the first domestic oven to be installed in a private house in the town.

Jet jewellery production was now carried out on a commercial scale, having begun around the year 1800, when a publican, John Carter of Haggersgate and a painter, Robert Jefferson, worked together in order to manufacture jet beads and trinkets, by hand, in Carter's premises. A retired gentleman known as Captain Tremlett visited the public house and saw the men at work, and showed them some amber beads made on a lathe, asking if jet could be turned in the same manner. It was then that Matthew Hill, who owned a woodturner's lathe, was brought on to the scene. Hill managed to produce beads on his machinery and was subsequently employed by a silversmith and druggist, Mr. Thomas Yeoman, to manufacture them on a commercial basis. The industry quickly grew and improved until, by the end of the 1800s, it had become so large that there was barely a single family in the town which did not have at least one member connected with the jet trade in some way. Royalty from around the world patronised a number of the town's jet dealers. Thomas Andrew supplied Queen Victoria with all her jet jewellery during the long period of mourning for her husband Albert, whilst Isaac Greenbury provided bracelets for the Empress of France.

By now Whitby had a number of amenities. The town's first library was established in Haggersgate in 1801, on the first floor of the *Star Inn*, whilst a little further down the street by 1827 stood the town's first public baths and museum.

In 1830 the tower of Whitby Abbey collapsed, only a day after a local chimney-sweep had won a bet by climbing it in order to retrieve the copper weather vane. The abbey structure had become a quarry by this time, with stones and other materials being used by all and sundry. This state of affairs continued until 1930, when the ruin was placed under the protection of the Ministry of Buildings and Works.

Shortly after yet another replacement bridge in 1835, whaling declined as quickly as it had begun, and by 1840 the town had found other uses for its sturdy ships: Cuffy and Duffy, the leaders of the Irish Rebellion in 1848, were transported along with other convicts in the locally built ships belonging to Stephen Wharton. The period between 1750 and 1850 saw Whitby become the principal port on the north-east coast. Shipbuilders and owners were in great demand, and a number of government transport service vessels were commissioned from the town's stocks. During the wars with the French, and in the American Civil War, Whitby-built vessels had also played their part. Emigrants for Quebec, and to a lesser extent for America, left by the thousand from the port in local vessels between 1831 and 1850. Indeed the Barrick shipyard manufactured comfortable ships especially for this purpose, including the *Columbus*, which sailed in April 1832 with 245 emigrants on board.

A new phase in the town's history was to come with the age of the railways. The West Cliff area was developed in the 19th century by George Hudson, the 'Railway King', and his investors, whose aim it was to develop the town as a fashionable spa resort. The railway originally came to Whitby from Pickering, thanks to George Stephenson, designer of the *Rocket*. It cost £80,000 and revolutionised the attitude of Whitby residents. Within a short time men, women and children, who had never travelled further than the other side of town, were able to break the bonds of isolation by travelling with relative ease to other parts of the kingdom. Horseback, coaches and even the sea, suddenly became less important as essential means of travel, and new ideas and attitudes began to infiltrate the formerly isolated community. Distinguished writers and artists were drawn to the town and a new income began to be generated from a growing stream of visitors.

Modern visitors to the town are surprised to find that Dracula is a local tourist attraction. The world famous vampire had his origins here, for he haunted the streets of this ancient port in the classic book written by Bram Stoker during one of his many stays in Whitby. Another master of fiction, Lewis Carroll, created part of *Alice in Wonderland* whilst on holiday here, and it is said that he composed *The Walrus and the Carpenter* verse whilst sunning himself on Whitby beach. The list of literary figures who over the years have left their mark, both on the town and the wider world, is lengthy and impressive, including Charles Dickens, George Du Maurier, Elizabeth Gaskell and local writers Storm Jameson and Leo Walmsley.

The year 1861 brought one of the worst disasters in the history of Whitby. During the great storm of that year many ships ran aground or began to sink as they desperately tried to head for the safety of Whitby harbour. Time and time again the rowing lifeboat returned to port with survivors, only to be relaunched yet again to answer another call. The crew were wet, cold and weary, yet despite their own problems they insisted on returning repeatedly to the aid of their fellow mariners. During one of these trips, and within calling distance of their loved ones watching from the pier, the lifeboat caught a large wave and overturned. Only one man in the lifeboat's crew, Henry Freeman, a bricklayer turned fisherman, survived. His survival was due to a new type of cork life-jacket which differed from those worn by the other crew members. The jacket became the prototype for all future lifeboat crews, and Freeman himself became something of a celebrity, having his picture complete with life-jacket used on a well-known brand of sardines. In 1881 the brave Whitby men showed their mettle once more, when they dragged the lifeboat eight miles overland, through a snowstorm, to rescue a stricken crew in Robin Hood's Bay.

Just 10 years after the terrible disaster of 1861, Whitby's first iron-built ship, the *Whitehall*, was launched amidst great optimism for the future of the shipyards. Problems were already becoming evident, however, as it was realised that the town as a shipbuilding port had its limitations. These became clearer still in 1887 when the first steel ship, the *Dora*, was launched. By this time newly-designed ships were too wide to fit the narrow bridge entrance, and in 1902 the Whitehall shipyard closed, leading to an exodus of 3,000 construction workers from the town. Shipbuilding has continued into modern times, though the size of the vessels ordered has diminished over the years. The recently sold Whitehall Shipyard is now planned as a site for a new sewerage development, whilst the Barrick, Langbourne and other yards have vanished under a new supermarket and marina development.

The 20th century has not greatly altered Whitby. The port still acts as a shelter for vessels seeking refuge from the fierce northerly gales which sweep this coast, though maritime disasters such as the long remembered wreck of the *Rohilla* are thankfully few. The hospital ship *Rohilla* came aground at Saltwick in 1914. Despite being within easy reach of the crowds on shore, many lives were lost as the desperate occupants of the ship attempted to swim the short distance to safety.

The modern bridge, opened on 24 July 1909, still regularly opens in bad weather to allow the fishing fleet into the upper harbour to shelter from the fierce northerly gales, as it has done for centuries, though Whitby's modern fleet is necessarily much smaller than it was in the herring boom of the 1950s. Diminishing fish stocks and E.E.C. quotas often make it more profitable to take out fishing parties of tourists, rather than to catch fish in the traditional manner.

Whitby now moves cautiously into the 21st century, but in doing so has not forgotten its historic roots. Change is slow, and modern development is monitored with an eagle eye by each and every resident. The future is important to Whitby, but so is the past, and few places in modern Britain offer such a balanced compromise between the two.

In writing the first words of this introduction, I stated that few towns could match Whitby's diversity of historical connections, or its list of notable residents and visitors. In writing these last few sentences, I realise to what extent these words are true. I have found it difficult to compress this vast history into so small a space, and necessity has ruled that vast subjects have received only a few words of description, or have been omitted altogether.

In the pages that follow I have attempted to capture at least a little of the atmosphere of Whitby in days gone by. I hope that readers familiar with the town will find that the pictures and information add to their interest and pleasure. I hope too that those who have not yet visited the town may gain an insight into its past, and will be spurred on to discover its many historical delights for themselves.

1. These 1910 sketches show the four sides of the shaft of Hawsker Cross, which was made of local stone. The six-and-a-half foot high cross shaft dates from the Viking age and at that time displayed typical ring knot and braid ornamentation, now much weathered.

2. Whitby Abbey as it appeared in 1773. The great central tower fell in 1830, after a chimney sweep had climbed it for a bet. A local tale tells of a small boy on the west side of the town who actually saw the tower fall and who told his parents, only to be rewarded with a 'thick ear' for telling lies.

3. This engraving, which depicts the abbey cross, shows it as it appeared in the early 1800s. Opinions are divided as to whether it was the 'Great Cross', mentioned as being in the abbey graveyard, or whether in fact it was only a market cross.

4. A street, a hospital, a school and two local churches, perpetuate the name of St Hilda, Whitby Abbey's first abbess. She is depicted here as modern eyes see her, and as she appeared on the actual seal or 'bulla' of Whitby Abbey in 1539.

Whitby Abbey.

5. The abbey and the abbey cross are pictured here in the days when the two were separated only by a wooden fence. Today a large wall separates abbey and cross. A modern road runs between the two and leads to a council car-park on the Abbey Plain. The whole area is under consideration for extensive excavations.

6. The parish church of St Mary, as it appeared *c.*1862. During the landslips of Henrietta Street in the 1870s, a large portion of the cliff and its pathway fell away, exposing to view coffins in the cliff side.

7. A rather imaginative portrait of the vision of Caedmon at Whitby Abbey, in which an angel appeared to ask him to sing of the creation. Caedmon, the 'Father of English Poetry and Song', is believed to have existed, although the tales surrounding his age, background and life style have become somewhat exaggerated and confused over the years.

8. St Mary's parish church and Caedmon's cross. Though the picture was taken in 1914, the scene is little changed, other than that many of the ancient tombstones have now become unreadable. In addition, a second large doorway was discovered in recent years beyond the porch in the picture. This has now been uncovered and restored.

9.   The quaint interior of St Mary's parish church, which dates from *c.*1110, looking towards the Cholmley pew and the three-decker pulpit. The church is still lit by candles. Its flat roof and box pews are a unique example of parochial workmanship, and a tribute to the craftsmen of the town.

10.   Though this print is dated 1842, it is believed that the sketch may have been made some years before. It shows Whitby and the abbey from the old Scarborough Road, now a backroad to Hawsker. Slightly to the left of the abbey can be seen the tower of St Mary's church, with remnants of the former pitched roof.

London. J & F. Harwood.

11.   A solitary steam vessel wends its way between sailing vessels in Whitby harbour in this fine 19th-century print. Union Mill can be seen in the distance, whilst in the foreground is a wide path. This path and the cliffs beyond have now fallen into the sea, to be replaced by a new walk along the present cliff edge.

12. The East Cliff close to St Mary's parish church. At the bottom right of the picture is Haggerlythe, the extreme end of Henrietta Street. It was this part of the town which on a number of occasions suffered major landslips, throwing homes and other buildings into the sea.

13. This panorama of Whitby's east side dates from *c.*1880. To the left of the picture is what remains of Henrietta Street after the landslips of the 1870s, when a methodist chapel, a pipe factory and other buildings and houses fell into the harbour. The white misaligned building (centre left) now marks the furthest extent of present buildings.

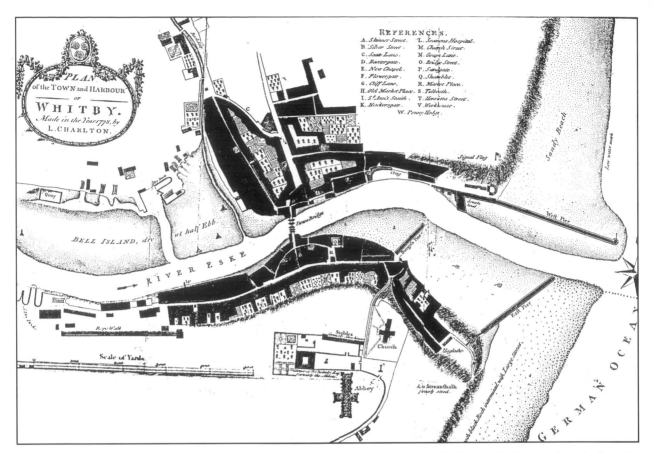

14. Whitby was a much more compact place in 1778 when this plan was drawn up. The fish pier had not yet been built and Bagdale beck, now covered by a road, was still an open river. In addition, there was no road directly to the pier from the bridge, and the West Cliff area was still fields.

15. The first bridge over the Esk was recorded in 1350, and others were built in 1610, 1766, 1835 and 1910. This engraving shows the bridge as it appeared in 1833, when it was proving too narrow for the movement of ships into the upper harbour, and was preventing the building of larger vessels in the town's shipyards.

16 & 17. Whitby's 'new' swivel bridge of 1835 was a much more robust structure than its predecessor. It is shown here both in a romanticised engraving made at the time, seen from the lower harbour, and in a later photograph, looking down-river from the south.

18. The well-to-do gentleman pictured leaning against the harbourside fence is said to be a former fisherman, John Hodgson. John was rowing a boat under Whitby Bridge one day, when he caught and returned a purse accidentally dropped by a lady above. On her death the lady was said to have left him a great deal of money.

19. A great storm sweeps Whitby harbour in the late 1800s, swamping the piers and quayside. In the distance can be seen the old bridge, over which is passing a rather windswept cart pulled by two horses. The high block of buildings to the immediate right of the bridge no longer exists.

20.   The old drawbridge and the entire block of buildings to the left of this scene have now disappeared. The buildings contained various businesses including Gray's Drapers. In later years Boot's the chemist bought property here, and the name 'Boot's Corner' came into being, a title that still exists, even though no corner of any sort is to be found here now.

21.   Ted Griffin, reputedly one of the town's tallest men, was photographed in 1908 while working on the demolition of Whitby's old bridge. Taken by Frank Meadow Sutcliffe, the noted photographer, this was evidently intended to show Griffin's height compared with the post behind him. Workmen can be seen on a temporary bridge in the background.

22. The opening of the present bridge, 24 July 1909. The temporary bridge used during its construction can be seen immediately behind it.

23. A recent local press campaign asked, 'what happened to our crown?'. The crown in question was displayed on Whitby bridge during the peace celebrations after the First World War. Locals were shocked to realise that the well-remembered crown was over 70 years old. This picture shows the illuminated bridge and its crown in 1919.

24. This photograph which depicts the present bridge, therefore dating from after 1909, shows an old sailing ship passing from the upper harbour to the lower, through the open bridge. Even in 1910 such ships were becoming rare. Beyond the bridge can be seen the now demolished buildings along Church Street's riverside.

25. The *Cap Palos* was a Canadian-built vessel which ran aground off the Whitby coastline. It was later refloated and brought into the harbour. The large building to its left was then the local headquarters of The Scarborough & Whitby Breweries.

CERTIFICATE OF DISCHARGE

FOR SEAMEN DISCHARGED BEFORE THE SUPERINTENDENT OF A MERCANTILE MARINE OFFICE IN THE UNITED KINGDOM, A BRITISH CONSUL, OR A SHIPPING OFFICER IN BRITISH POSSESSION ABROAD.

SANCTIONED BY THE BOARD OF TRADE JANUARY, 1869.

No. 81

Name of Ship.	Offici. Number.	Port of Registry	Regist.d Tonnage.
Joseph & Mayner	44473	Whitby	211

Horse Power of Engines (if any)	Description of Voyage or Employment.
	Foreign

Name of Seaman.	Age.	Place of Birth.	No of R.N.R. Commiss.n or Certif.	Capacity. If Mate or Engineer No of Certif (if any)
William Barrett	23	Whitby	—	A.B

Date of Engagement.	Place of Engagement.	Date of Discharge.	Place of Discharge.
16th March	10ee Hartpool	8 02 June	Kirkcaldy

I certify that the above particulars are correct, and that the above named Seaman was discharged accordingly: and that the character described on the other side hereof is a true copy of the Report concerning the said Seaman.

Dated this 9 day of June 1870.

Richard Porter .... MASTER.

AUTHENTICATED BY

W.B. Pethie

SIGNATURE OF SUPERT. CONSUL, OR SHIPPING OFFICER.

OFFICE SEAL OR OFFICIAL STAMP KIRKCALDY 9

Signature of Seaman

NOTE Any Person who makes, assists in making or procures to be made any false Certificate or Report of the Service Qualifications, Conduct, or Character of any Seaman, or who forges, assists in forging, or procures to be forged, or fraudulently alters, assists in fraudulently altering, or procures to be fraudulently altered, any such Certificate or Report, or who fraudulently makes use of any Certificate or Report, or of any Copy of any Certificate or Report which is forged or altered or does not belong to him, shall for each such offence be deemed guilty of a misdemeanor and may be fined or imprisoned.

26. Whitby has a long tradition of sailors and seamanship. The sailor's discharge certificate which dates from 1870 relates to William Barrett, then aged 23, and gives details of the sailor and his ship. The section of the certificate headed 'Horse power of engines (if any)' is left blank, indicating that the vessel was a sailing ship.

27. Whitby's upper harbour scene has changed a great deal from the days when the wooden quay at the left of the picture existed. To the right of the yacht on the far side of the river can be seen a wide slipway. This was Alders Waste, believed to be the site of the town's earliest Viking settlement.

28. Early days at Dock End, *c*.1900. The dock area was later partly filled in to form a car-park, but in recent years has been completely redeveloped, and a road now stretches as far as the ships in the foreground.

29. Another view of Dock End. To the left is the old wooden quay with the *Angel Hotel Vaults*. These were demolished when New Quay Road was built. The distinctive Friendship Rowing Club boat house, which can be seen in the centre of the picture, is still in existence.

30.   Steam trawlers moored at the old quay on Pier Road, *c*.1900

31.   The Spital Bridge ropery is shown here as it was at the turn of the century. In its heyday, much of the rigging for Whitby's sailing ships would have been manufactured here. The timber pond in the foreground is now silted up, and the ropery buildings are gone.

32. Before the new quayside was built, the area from the bridge to the pier was virtually the same width as St Ann's Staith, whose name was applied to its full length. Following the widening of this lower area, the name remained for the upper part whilst the rest became known as Pier Road.

33. St Ann's Staith as it appeared in 1906. Houses were once built on both sides of this street, but were demolished in the days before photography. The *Buck* and *Jolly Sailors* public houses on the left are still in existence, though the garage and cycle shop between have been taken over by the expansion of the *Jolly Sailors*.

34. An early 1900s scene of Whitby's harbourside is depicted in this old postcard. It is interesting to note that small craft still predominate, and only one fishing boat with a wheelhouse appears on the scene.

35. This photographic study, entitled 'Why hasn't the boat come back?', captures the essence of fear and worry on the faces of fishermen's wives, waiting at the pier head for an overdue fishing boat. The three Whitby women are not named, but their dress is typical of that worn by women of the fishing community at the turn of the century.

36. One of Whitby's 'old sea-dogs'. He is seen wearing the traditional fisherman's jersey or Gansey. Each town and village had its own pattern, and each family had a distinctive variation on the standard design. The reason for this was practical rather than decorative, as it acted as an aid to identification in cases of shipwreck and drowning.

37. Another group of locals from the fishing community awaits the return of the fishing boats. The headscarf and full ankle-length skirts with 'pinny' are typical of the hundred years up to the early 1950s. The picture is taken on the old wooden quay of the west pier. The long wooden rail at ground level is to allow for the movement of ships' ropes.

38.   The timeless quality of the coble fisherman's way of life is captured in this photograph. The fishermen are seen gathering in their nets as they have done for centuries, and as they do to this very day. In the background can be seen the cliffs on the western side of town. These have been restabilised in recent years to prevent erosion.

39.   The 1,139-ton *Isle of Iona* photographed just before it broke up on Whitby Rock on 7 December 1906. The site of the wreck was literally within shouting distance of the town's east pier, and is now covered by the pier extension, completed *c.*1910.

WRECK SALE

WILL BE AUCTIONED PUBLICLY

AT THE

WHALER'S ARMS INN, WHITBY

at 10 o'clock in the forenoon on

THURSDAY, DECEMBER 13th 1828

the remaining cargo and effects of the Schooner "BOUNTY," Master, Gabriel Stranton, which foundered on Whitby Sand in a great storm on the 8th day of September. 1828. on route to London the following goods, whole or partly damaged, consisting of:-

Dried Fish, Oak Planking, Whale Oil, Iron Flax, Hemp

1400 Staves, Ashes, Sailcloth

115 pieces of exceeding fine oak timber and a few oak handspikes

3000 Oakpipe and hogshead staves

400 Pieces of fine oak timber. Rope and ships fittings.

40. Wreck sales were an unfortunate consequence of the many shipwrecks off Whitby's rocky coastline. Much 'wrecking', or looting, from wrecks also took place. There appears to be no trace of a *Whalers Arms Inn* ever having existed in the town in 1828, though the name could have been a colloquialism for a local tavern.

41. The *Illustrated London News* of 11 October 1851 carried a picture and a report of the wrecks of the *Mary* and *Hope*, which were coal carriers belonging to the town. Behind can be seen the coastguard station on Battery Parade, now incorporated into the present buildings on that site, and now used as café premises.

42. This rare picture shows the hospital ship *Rohilla* as she was before she was wrecked near Whitby in October 1914. The once magnificent ship broke to pieces within a short time, and many lives were lost. One of the survivors, Mrs. Keziah Mary Roberts, had also survived the sinking of the *Titanic* two years earlier.

43. Remains of the bridge of the *Rohilla*, photographed shortly after the wreck. Also to be seen in the picture is the wrecked number two lifeboat, which was holed during the rescue attempts. A number of wooden items, from lace bobbins to large tables and chairs and from paperknives to writing cabinets, exist in the town which were carved from driftwood from the wreck.

44. A group taken locally, *c*.1914. The central figure is known to be a Whitby sea-scout named R. Jewitt, born 1898, though the rest of the group are unnamed. It is believed the men, and perhaps the nurses also, are survivors of the wreck of the *Rohilla*.

45. The rowing lifeboat is seen here on its wheeled cradle, which would be manually pulled to the slipway before launching. The slipway is situated slightly to the right, just out of the picture, whilst on the left of the photograph is the old lifeboat shed, seen in the days before the town's yacht club was built on its flat roof.

46. In this picture Whitby's old rowing lifeboat is being launched from its wheeled cradle on Whitby beach, near Battery Parade.

47. Henry Freeman, the sole survivor of the 1861 lifeboat disaster. Freeman was a bricklayer turned fisherman and was the 13th member of the crew, a fact which was well noted by the superstitious members of the community. Freeman's life was saved by the new cork lifejacket.

48. The gloomy interior of Whitby's old fish market on the west pier. Hundreds of fish are laid out neatly in rows ready for sale, whilst a fisherman smoking a clay pipe is silhouetted against the bright sunshine outside. The old wooden railings which separated the dual-level pier further along can be seen in the background.

49. No tide at the bar! An extremely rare early 1900s photograph of Whitby harbour in a completely dry state. The photograph is taken between the piers, close to the harbour bar, with the fishermen walking on the dry river bed. The objects on their heads are long-lines, a type of fishing line, once common.

50. These five local fishermen were photographed on Tate Hill Pier with one of the hand-made crab pots whose design has not changed to the present day. The man with the crab pot is believed to be a Mr. Forden, whilst the others are identified as (from left to right): Mr. Peart, Mr. Leadley, William 'Ploshers' Barratt, and 'Old Cud' Colley Walker.

51. Penzancemen was the general name given to the Cornish fishing boats which were frequent visitors to the port in the 19th and early 20th centuries. This rare picture of the fleet at anchor off the coast includes a number of these Cornish vessels, as well as a lone rowing boat, obviously taking advantage of the calm conditions.

52. This picture captures one ancient Penzanceman, moored alongside the old wooden quay at 'Dock End'. This area has now been filled in and constitutes New Quay Road, and the roundabout of a new road system leading to Whitby Marina.

53. A typical Whitby 'keel boat' *c.*1890 is seen here set against a backdrop of sailing ships and mud flats. The Bell Shoal, as the mud island was known, has now been cleared away. Captain Cook's ships were built around this area of the riverside, which has subsequently been reclaimed and developed into a marina and supermarket.

54. Photographed in the early 1900s, this pair of 'old sea dogs' chat of days gone by. The man on the left constructs a traditional crab pot from material held in a tin bath, whilst to his right his companion rests his knee against a wooden barrel once used for the transport of fresh fish by road.

55. A delightful portrait in the early 1900s of a Whitby fish seller and her customer. The photograph is believed to have been taken on The Cragg, now a narrow footpath running parallel to Pier Road, but once the only road connecting the town and Scotch Head. The empty doorway shows interesting decorative wall tiles and a slot in which a 'baby-gate' could be inserted.

56. A local fisherman poses with his prize catch in the old fish shed on Pier Road.

57. Between the wars, fishermen's wives would supplement their income by setting up stalls on the pier selling fishing lines, mussels for bait and similar items. These two stalls were to be found almost opposite the *Fisherman's Tavern*, a public house which has now become café premises.

58. With the decline of the fishing industry, only tales remain of the days when it is said one could walk from one side of the harbour to the other on the decks of moored fishing boats. This picture of *c.*1950 captures the time when French, Belgian, Dutch and other foreign boats competed with the English and Scottish herring fleet for harbour space.

59. The power of the tide has long since washed away the cliff which used to connect with the east-side pier. A number of temporary structures (known as Spa Ladders) have bridged the gap over the years, being replaced as often as new cliff falls dictated. A modern concrete bridge stands in place of this early wooden structure.

60. Precisely dated 29 January 1863, this engraving gives an artist's impression of the approach to Whitby harbour from the sea. The extensions had not yet been added to the piers, and an early paddle steamer can be seen heading for port.

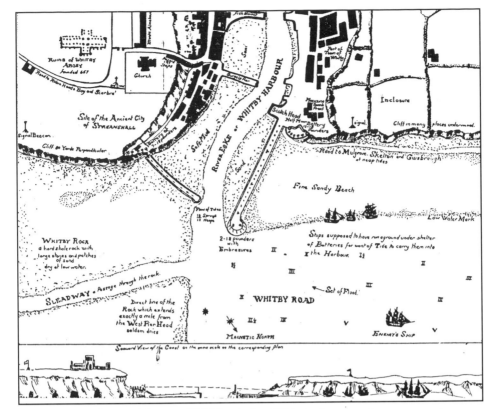

61. A map of the sea defences of Whitby during 1794. At that time there were twelve 18-pounder cannons at the western battery (still called Battery Parade), and seven 18-pounders on the east side. Two additional cannons were also in place at the end of the pier. It is interesting to note the beach road to Guisborough.

62. The piers from the evocatively named Khyber Pass and Spion Kop. Khyber Pass is the artificial cutting connecting Pier Road with the West Cliff area. The ridge to the right is known as Spion Kop. Though the postcard carries the date 29 July 1911, the picture is already out of date, for the pier extensions, missing in the photograph, would have been completed by this date. In the centre of the picture is the former coastguard station with its high lookout tower.

63. Whitby's 'Walking Men' which have gone down in local folklore are seen here *c*.1909. The name stems from the structures which were used to build the pier extensions, and which literally walked along the sea-bed during the process of construction.

64. This group are believed to be Whitby coastguards and customs officials. The picture was taken by local photographer W. Herbert of Baxtergate and the date, 5 August 1892, was carefully noted on the back. Unfortunately the names of the sitters were not also recorded.

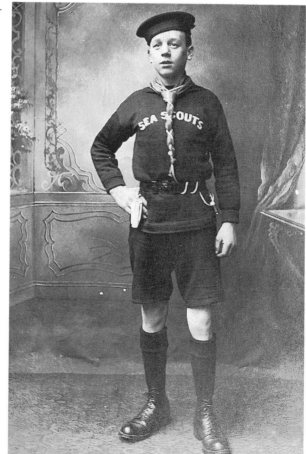

65. In the days when photography was still new, each and every major event in one's life would be recorded at the local studio if one could afford the photographer's fees. This proud young sea-scout had probably just received his new uniform, and his parents would no doubt have had prints made for all the family.

66 & 67. These two husband and wife portraits, by local photographer W. H. Heming, illustrate two different life-styles co-existing within the town in the late 19th century. Heming's original studio in Henrietta Street fell into the sea during a landslip in either 1870 or 1873. He later moved to new premises in Pier Road.

68. At Christmas in 1912, Captain and Mrs. Kirby sent this photograph with a printed Christmas greeting to their friends Mr. and Mrs. Willis of Red House, Easington, Saltburn. Captain and Mrs. Kirby are pictured with family and servants outside Sunnylea, Chubb Hill. The road was at that time the residence of businessmen and sea captains.

69. Sail manufacture was a profitable business in the late 1860s, allowing a number of quite ordinary people to become wealthy businessmen. Their new prosperity enabled them to invest in a number of other trades, thereby increasing their wealth further. One such man was William Roe who lived in Bagdale, and is seen pictured here with his family.

Brotherhood of the F.B.I.

Lat 64° 24' N.   Lo 21° 28' W

All Mankind, Wherever Ye May Be, Greetings Know All Ye Men By These Presents, that _Robert Dugill R.B._ of the _Royal Navy_ in the good ship _R.M.S. Sprayville_ is hereby initiated into the mysterious terrors of and forevermore elected to the great Brotherhood of the F.B.I. having entered and endured the requisite period of one hundred and one days or longer in the domain of and waters adjacent to ICELAND.

Signed _____ GREAT COD

Pr. Sheriff Lieut Com. RNR CAPTAIN

Signed _____ GRAND EIDER

70. Arctic waters were once as familiar to some Whitby men as the North Sea was to others. Whalers and other vessels often marked long voyages to these waters by a special on-board ceremony, similar to that which took place when crossing the equator. This undated certificate shows the continuity of the custom. The letters F.B.I. probably mean Frozen B......s in Iceland!

71. Captain William Scoresby joined a Whitby whaler in 1785 and within six years had been appointed a captain. He made about 30 voyages to the Arctic, catching over 533 whales. He died in 1829.

72. This 'Japanese shogun' gentleman is in fact a local resident of *c.*1890. The photograph, which was taken in Yokohama, would possibly have been brought home as a souvenir, following a trip on one of Whitby's many sailing ships.

73. A prominent Quaker community once existed in the town, particularly among those involved in businesses, such as banking and shipping. This portrait, believed to be of a Mr. Dryden, illustrates a style of clothing and beard often associated with Quaker men.

74. A Whitby postman, no doubt having just been given his uniform, posed for a Carte de Visite portrait at the studios of Tom Watson, a renowned local photographer. Watson, who lived at Lythe, one of the villages on the outskirts of the town, was known for his documentary style of photography.

75. William Sawdon was a well-known Whitby watchmaker and jeweller, who had premises at 20 Bridge Street in 1899. This portrait of William and his wife Eleanor appears not to have been taken at a studio, but possibly at 2 Esk Terrace, his home.

76. One of the town's biggest fires swept through a group of buildings at the junction of Bridge Street and Sandgate on 6 March 1912. The picture shows the destroyed Tyler's shoe shop which suffered the same fate as Nicholson ironmongers, Loraine's hairdressers and Anderson's clothiers.

77. Clarkson & Son, glovers and silk mercers, owned these properties at the end of the 19th century. They stood at the junction of Grape Lane, close to the end of the bridge over the River Esk. The premises were demolished at the turn of the century, and the present *Dolphin Hotel*, situated behind in Grape Lane, was rebuilt.

78. In 1864 the election was a riotous affair. These ruffians were engaged as special constables in order to control the fierce rivalry which existed between opposing factions.

79. Even in early times, Whitby was proud of its heritage. This picture of a Church Street souvenir shop in the early 1900s shows windows crammed with postcards, large prints and other views of the area. In addition, baskets, wooden spades, wooden boats and trains are all to be found displayed in the shop window.

80. The coronation of King George V in 1910 gave the loyal people of Whitby a chance to celebrate in the traditional manner. This picture taken of Johnson's pork butcher's shop in Church Street is typical of the enthusiastic way in which such decoration was undertaken by the occupants of individual premises.

81. Another royal occasion prompted the owners of W. Hunter's premises, at 4 Skinner Street, to pose with staff outside their decorated shop. The two young boys seen each side of the shop were probably bystanders, and were perhaps never intended to appear in the photograph!

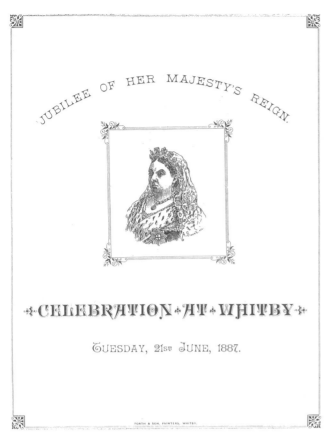

82. Queen Victoria was a patron of the Whitby jet jewellery manufacturers during her long period of mourning for her husband Albert. During the jubilee celebrations of 1887 the Whitby people celebrated their loyalty with processions through the town, street parties, and much general rejoicing.

83. An exquisite example of the art of Whitby jet craftsmen, the chessboard made entirely of the local gemstone with inlaid local fossil ammonites. It was made by John Sherwood and took four years to complete. Elisha Walker (the writer's great grandfather), himself a jet merchant, is said to have bought it for £40 c.1870. It is now in private hands.

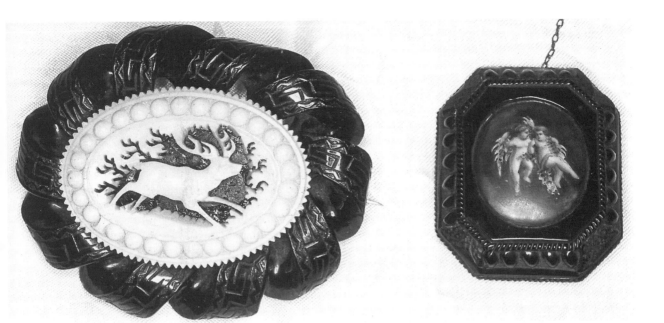

84. Two examples of Victorian
craftsmanship. On the left is a hand-
carved oval jet brooch with a white
stag inset of ivory, whilst on the right a
jet pendant contains a hand-painted
china inset.

85. Jet beads came in many shapes
and sizes. It was common practice in
the town for a person's position in the
family to be denoted by the number of
rows of beads worn. Children would
wear fewer rows than their elder sisters
or their mother, who in turn would
have fewer rows of beads than the
grandmother.

86. This photograph is believed to show the christening of the present Marquis of Normanby. Mulgrave Castle, the Marquis' home, lies on the outskirts of the town. It was on the lands of Mulgrave estate that alum mining took place, in the 17th and 18th centuries, and where, to this day, the remains of the industry can be detected in the cliffs at Sandsend.

87.   The alum industry. This picture is believed to show the alum works at Sandsend, close to the town, whilst the attached engravings from an earlier period show cloth being treated with alum, before the dyeing process.

88.   Whitby from Boghall. Before the railway came to Whitby in 1836, the road here continued to the right, connecting with an ancient ford over the river. Weighills tannery was situated in the buildings in the left foreground, c.1828. The purpose of the white flagpole-like structures, seen at regular intervals along both sides of Esk Terrace, has not been explained.

89. A distant view of Whitby showing the Prussian blue dye works which existed at Larpool up to the early 1900s, at the end of the town. The large chimney and buildings have now vanished, though blue stains can still be detected on the rocks in the area. A new high level road bridge now crosses the river beyond the chimney.

90. Rig Mill, on the outskirts of town, is now a private residence. A mill has existed at this spot since the early days of Whitby Abbey, *c*.1200, which it is believed to have served. An old paved 'monks trod' or packhorse road led to, and beyond, the mill. It can still be traced through woods and fields, but is now overgrown.

91. Cock Mill was a working water mill at the edge of town, where picnickers would gather on sunny summer afternoons in the 19th century. The mill has now become a private residence, and the grounds around it are no longer accessible to the public.

92. Grosmont village, a short distance from Whitby, is now a haven of rural peace. This engraving of 1860 shows a totally different scene, with smoke stacks and railway sidings belonging to the once prosperous iron works.

93. Though lacking in foreground detail, this early picture is interesting in that it represents a view of Whitby which cannot now be seen. The farmtrack on which the photographer stood, and the fields themselves, have now been taken over by the Abbots Road and Helredale housing estates.

NOTICE

1794

AN EXPRESS

STAGE COACH

from the

"White Horse and Griffin" Hotel,

WHITBY

and

Fox and Rabbit Arms, Malton village

WILL RUN

(if God permits)

stopping for refreshment, ale, exercise and Smoking,

the whole journey in 14 days

All that are desirous to pass to London Stamford or other Place on that Road; Let them repair to Henry Goodwood at the White Horse and Griffin.

Fare all Weights and Ages.

8 shillings outside   **15 shillings inside**

BEGINS ON THURSDAY, 9th APRIL,

Each person allowed 3 lbs. luggage,
No crossing, jostling, and kicking.
PIGS will be turned out.

All last wills should be made before departure.

94. Stagecoach journeys were not to be taken lightly in 1794, when the distance to London would seem like a trip to the end of the world. Even so, a period of 14 days in transit would seem excessive for an 'Express' service. No doubt the threat of highway robbery prompted the request for wills to be made before departure.

FOR

QUEBEC,

AND THE CANADAS,

With Goods & Passengers,

AND CARRIES A SURGEON:

THE FINE NEW SHIP

COLUMBUS,

BURTHEN 150 TONS,

H. BARRICK, COMMANDER;

WILL SAIL FROM WHITBY ABOUT THE FIRST WEEK IN

APRIL, 1832.

This Ship having a Poop and Forecastle, and 7ft 6in between Decks affords superior Accommodations for Passengers desirous to embark for America.

For Terms of Passage (the Ship finding Water and Fuel) and Freight of Goods, apply to Messrs H & G. BARRICK, Ship-Builders Whitby, who will give Letters of Recommendation to their Agent at Quebec; also, ample information respecting the employment of Labourers, and Small Capitalists for the Sale of Land in Upper Canada.

☞ Early applications are requested as the Ship is expected soon to be filled up.

R. RODGERS, PRINTER, WHITBY.

95.   Between 1831 and 1850, around 2,000 emigrants left the port of Whitby for Canada. The Barrick shipyard, which was on land now covered by the new Co-op supermarket development, began to build ships especially for emigrants. This poster gives details of one such ship, the *Quebec*.

96. This photograph, c.1920, of an unknown local man, returning from market with a live goose on his back, captures a time when life was simple and public transport was virtually unknown in the town. Farmers would often walk 10 or 15 miles to attend the Saturday market, and having bought or sold their wares would walk home again.

97. Around 1905-25 Wilcock's, the Whitby grocer had a weekly delivery service to rural areas. The two-horse delivery cart in the picture is being driven by a Mr. Simpson, whilst his assistant may well be Joe Akeroyd. The location has not been positively identified.

98.   Believed to be Whitby's first motor vehicle, this is a 12-horsepower Darracq, owned by
Mr. A. H. Walker, who was to build up a well-known garage business in the town. The two-cylinder
vehicle ran for a year before the registration number seen in the picture was issued. Mr. Walker's wife
Mabel, (née Gray) was apparently the town's first woman driver.

99.   Walker's garage on Royal Crescent became the centre of the early motor trade in Whitby. The area has now been
taken over by the Post Office, and the area sorting office now occupies a new building on the same site.

100. Workmen building the Whitby-Sandsend road. Construction was by manual labour, with the assistance of horse-powered vehicles. An earlier road was financed by Prince Duleep Singh who leased Mulgrave Castle (now the home of Lord Normanby). Duleep Singh belonged to Indian royalty; indeed his family once owned the famous Kohinoor diamond, now in the British crown jewels.

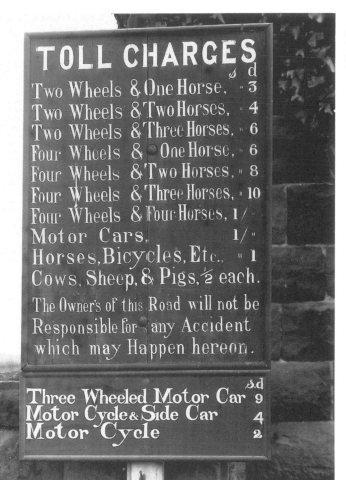

TOLL CHARGES

	s	d
Two Wheels & One Horse,	"	3
Two Wheels & Two Horses,	"	4
Two Wheels & Three Horses,	"	6
Four Wheels & One Horse,	"	6
Four Wheels & Two Horses,	"	8
Four Wheels & Three Horses,	"	10
Four Wheels & Four Horses,	1/	
Motor Cars,	1/	"
Horses, Bicycles, Etc.,	"	1
Cows, Sheep, & Pigs, ½ each.		

The Owners of this Road will not be Responsible for any Accident which may Happen hereon.

	s	d
Three Wheeled Motor Car		9
Motor Cycle & Side Car		4
Motor Cycle		2

101 & 102. The newly-built route between Whitby and Sandsend remained privately owned for some time. The pictures show the gate which barred the road at the toll booth, now a private dwelling, and the toll charges as they were until 1922.

103.   Until a road was constructed between Whitby and Sandsend, travel along this stretch of the coastal route was by the beach. In later years the toll road was built, to be superseded by a new, improved highway in 1925. This picture taken near White Point bridge shows the opening ceremony.

104.   Advertisement for Milburn's motor 'Chars-a-Banc'.

105. Following the end of the First World War, motor transport came into its own, and charabanc trips became a popular event. This unknown group is believed to have booked for one of the many tours organised by Milburn's Motor 'Chars-a-Banc'.

106. After the First World War, ex-government vehicles were bought and used by tradesmen and local authorities. This Foden steam wagon is one such vehicle. It was bought by the county council and was driven between Whitby and Scarborough by Mr. Jim Chambers who is seen leaning against the vehicle. It is parked outside Scalby railway station.

107.   A later photograph of a group of Whitby tourists, this time believed to be on a trip to Pickering.

108. Haggersgate was a narrow place before the demolition of property in the 1950s made it the width we see today. This extremely short street originally had five public houses: the *Star*, the *Elephant and Castle*, the *Neptune*, the *Steam Packet*, and the *Ship*. All had entrances on to the street. Today only the *Star* and *Ship* remain.

109. The bridge in this picture indicates that the photograph was taken before 1909. It shows a group of boys, whose only playground was the beach and harbourside. This area has been overtaken by an extension to Pier Road, whilst the sand is now covered by black mud.

110. Whitby fish market at Coffee House End. Though the name is no longer in current use, this area of Pier Road still exists, and is close to the present covered fish market. The well-dressed group is probably connected with Turner's fish merchants, though the central character with the bowler hat is known to be local butcher Fred Clough.

FISH SALE. WHITBY.

111.   Another scene at Whitby's old fish market. The building marked W. Eglon was formerly the *Neptune* public house, which was closed in 1904 at the request of the police. The picture is particularly interesting because of the wide variety of dress and headgear worn by those in the crowd.

112.   This view from St Ann's Staith was taken before 1909, from the window of what was then a brewery. The corner building on the right, with the white upper section, belonged to Gray's the drapers. It was later taken over by Boot's the chemist, and became known as Boot's Corner. The name remains to this day, though all buildings are gone.

113.   This quaint scene of Whitby's Old Market Place in 1818, looking towards the drawbridge and the abbey beyond, was taken from a fire-cloth on the stage of one of the town's old theatres. The scene is greatly changed since all the buildings beyond the first block (on the right and left of the picture) have disappeared.

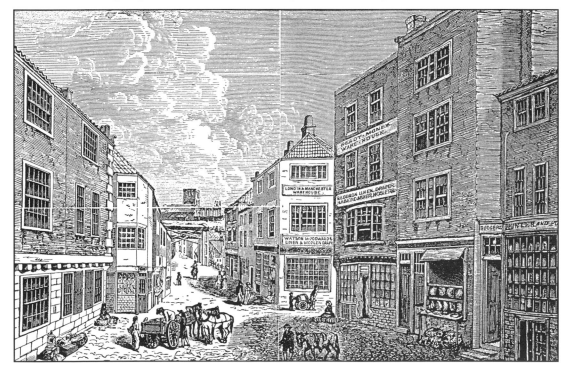

114. In the early 1800s Whitby's east side had a greater density of dwellings than it has today. Many of these were pulled down under slum clearance schemes. Other properties have vanished over the years, including St Michael's church (centre), and virtually the whole of Church Street's riverside buildings to its right.

115. St Michael's church, as it would have appeared from the harbourside in the 1940s. The row of houses (top left) is Aelfleda Terrace, named after one of St Hilda's pupils, Princess Aelfleda, who succeeded her teacher as abbess of Whitby Abbey. Virtually all the other buildings in the background have now been demolished.

116. Described on this old postcard as 'A bit of old Whitby', Tin Ghaut was a narrow alleyway which sloped from Grape Lane on Whitby's east side to the harbour. The ancient buildings were pulled down in the 1960s despite local protests, and the area has now been turned into a car-park by Scarborough Borough Council.

117. Tin Ghaut, seen here from its junction with Grape Lane. Ghauts are a local peculiarity. The word derives from the Viking word Gat, meaning way or road. All Ghauts start at street level and descend gradually to the harbour. Tin Ghaut is said to derive its name from the local dialect (T'inn Ghaut), meaning that an inn once stood here.

118.   Who knows what feats of achievement were realised in later life by this generation of Whitby schoolchildren? This class of 1905 is from St Michael's school, situated close to the harbourside in Church Street. It was demolished in the 1960s, along with St Michael's church, and a whole range of other buildings.

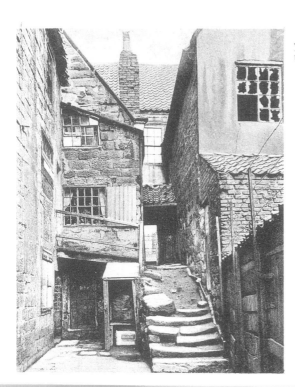

119. Argument's Yard, shown in a dilapidated state in 1918. The yard, which takes its name from a family who once owned the property there, is typical of the many alleys which lead down to the harbourside.

120. A lack of space round Whitby's harbourside meant that galleried tenements were common. Those on Boulby Bank, now demolished and much mourned by the town's residents, were perhaps the best, and virtually the last, example in the town. Their final days in the 1950s were captured in this photograph, which shows children at a tap which provided the only running water.

121. Wilson's Yard was one of the many narrow alleyways leading off Church Street, which contained rows of galleried houses. The fisherman, seen here in the early 1900s mending his nets, would probably have lived in one of the houses on the wooden walkway above, whilst storing his fishing equipment in the room at ground level below.

122. The picture taken in Church Street, is from an old photographic catalogue. A scribbled note on the top of the sheet identifies one of the women as 'Mrs. Midwoods, the mint manufacturer'. She could possibly be the wife of Peter Midwood, who is known to have lived on Tate Hill, Church Street, in 1899.

123.   The Toll Booth or Old Town Hall, was built by Nathaniel Cholmley in 1788. The market square which it surveys still hosts a weekly Saturday market and has been re-cobbled in recent years to resemble once more the scene as depicted in the print. The stocks which were said to exist close by have never been replaced.

124.   Appleton Stephenson was a local solicitor who, prior to 1837, set up the Esk Brewery in Church Street. This engraving shows the brewery as it appeared at that time. The building has now been replaced by a wholesale fruit and vegetable warehouse, though Brewery Yard close by still exists.

125.   The scene at St Ann's Staith has changed a lot since this photograph was taken just after the First World War. The fountain has been moved, whilst the *Red Lion* public house has been pulled down, making way for Woolworth's store. In the mid-1800s, a row of shops and houses on the harbour side of the street was demolished.

126. Mislabelled 'The Cliffs, Whitby', an old postcard shows the tranquil harbour scene around the lifeboat shed. The building to its immediate right was originally an indoor market, but since about 1942 it has been used as a clothing factory. The building is on the original site of the Shambles, a group of butchers' shops and slaughter-houses.

127. With the increase of shipbuilding in the port, the authorities found it necessary to ensure that the river channel was kept from silting up. This picture shows an early wooden dredger moored alongside Whitehall shipyard.

128. Up to the mid-1700s, Bagdale Beck, which flows beneath the road at Bagdale, was an open river. Around 1920 severe rains caused the river to overflow, so that once more it flowed above the modern roadway. This scene shows Station Square, with what was then Howards Garage (left), and Arthur Sawdon's furniture stores (now an estate agent).

129. Loggerhead Yard, formerly Doctor Lane, takes its name from the ship's loggerhead, or figurehead, which is still to be seen on a café in Baxtergate. The café was formerly the *Shiplaunch Inn, c.*1740-1915, and stands at the top of the yard. It was once connected with another public house at the other end of Loggerhead Yard by a smugglers' tunnel.

CHILDREN'S PEACE CELEBRATION,
WHITBY, JULY 16TH, 1919.

130.   Crowds gathered in the town's Station Square for the peace celebrations in July 1919. Recently the station, which can be seen to the left, has been restored by removing a number of wooden shops. These were added to its frontage in later years. The trees at the right have long since disappeared, and Whitby bus station now covers this area.

131. This early view of Station Square is almost unrecognisable compared with the present scene. The large house, right of centre, was the Central Restaurant when the picture was taken. It was formerly the railway stationmaster's house, and stood on the site of what is now the bus station.

132. This elaborate indoor scene with painted scenery and mock shop fronts would appear at first glance to be a stage set for some extravaganza. It is, in fact, the scene in one of Whitby's meeting halls during a fundraising bazaar of 1905.

133. Anyone for tennis? The Fishburn Park tennis club is pictured here *c.*1930 in front of what is believed to be the old nurses' quarters of Whitby Cottage Hospital. The nurses' quarters were demolished, and the whole area has now been completely enveloped by Whitby's new hospital complex.

134.   In 1911 photography was still an expensive process. Perhaps that is why that this photograph was given as a 'first prize with honours' to each of the winners of the Eskdale Tournament of Song pictured here. The Tournament of Song still takes place each year in the town.

135.   Members of the North Riding Royal Engineers V Signal Company, No. 3 section, gather for a photograph while at Whitby during the years of the First World War.

136.   Looking something like a pair of extras from an early silent movie, these two local 'boys at the front' are identifiable only from their enigmatic placard, which labels them simply, 'Rich & Co.'.

137.   It is not known if this soldier is a prisoner of war, or simply a serving soldier. What is evident is that the picture was taken 'somewhere in France' in November 1916. The man's name is possibly revealed by a message in pencil on the rear of the photograph, which reads 'Compliments F. McCarthy'.

Account of bombardment from the local newspaper dated 18 December 1914:

Like a bolt from the blue to the people of Whitby came the naval bombardment on Wednesday morning. It came when business and working people generallly had just got nicely settled down to the duties of the day. Bang-crash came the first shell, and, with the second boom and nerve-racking crash, every intelligent person was immediately impressed with the idea that the Germans had opened fire on the town. It was unlike anything they had ever heard overhead either in the way of thunder or shipwreck signal; and then for every two or three seconds of seven momentous minutes, four-inch shells were rained over the old town. With long-fixed calculation, the two fine cruisers had chosen their stand with such a nicety that every place and structure of importance – signal station, electric-power station, gasworks, and viaduct, came within their line of fire. The place selected for opening fire happened to be but a very short distance to the northward of the scene of the wreck of the hospital ship *Rohilla.* The warships first appeared round the bend of the cliffs three miles to the south of the harbour; they came through the foam and spume of an angry though wind-less sea, and dimmed by a haze which formed a fit backing for their evil work. How the men of Whitby – especially those who had handled the forty-pounder breech-loader gun which at one time was mounted on the cliffs, wished for something of the kind to reply with! There was a calm but indignant spirit shown by the men of Whitby; but the women, they were naturally distressed, because they did not fully comprehend the nature of the danger, and the best way to avoid it. Most people kept in their houses, though many showed a restless move towards the country. As a whole, the town stood the punishment with marvellous composure. The spirit of the men was typified by the young man who, immediately the ships steamed away, went off to the Recruiting Station to enlist. Doctors, The Devon Light Infantry, Police, and Ambulance Men were cool and collected and ready to call upon their energies. This incident of war – so disastrous to us as a town – was considered but as an incident in the great war which is testing the spirit of the nation. Admiral von Tirpitz makes a mistake if he thinks to hearten his Berlin friends by a demonstration of cowardice on the part of the people of Whitby. They snap their fingers at him, and ask him to send still more of his ships into the North Sea, that our Jacks may have a chance to send them to Davy Jones's locker. Very naturally our readers are anxious to know what has become of these particular warships, but all we seaboard people know how wide and free is the ocean and how difficult it must be to round up or make fight vessels possessing great powers of speed. Of course, it is presumed that they have come out of the Kiel Canal, and that their main object was a demonstration along the coast, so that they could wireless to the Kaiser: 'Hoch, hoch, we have invaded England, destroyed their big ports and shipping, now await attack by the British Grand Fleet, Hoch, hoch!' We have unbounded confidence in our fine old Admiral, whom we lovingly call 'Jacky Fisher', to deal in a seamanlike fashion with the enemy.

138. Outrage at the attack ensured that many locals swiftly signed up for army service. Recruitment posters such as this ensured that the incident was not quickly forgotten.

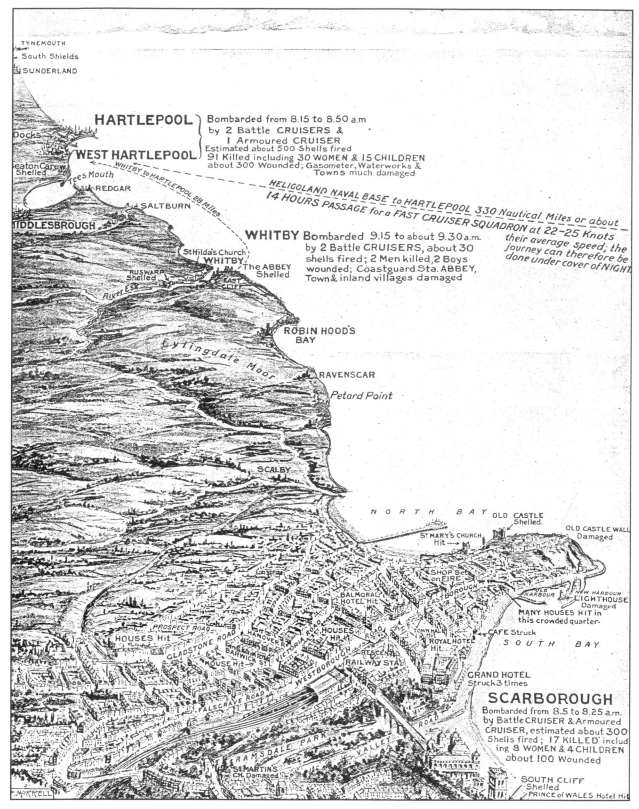

HARTLEPOOL } Bombarded from 8.15 to 8.50 a.m
WEST HARTLEPOOL } by 2 Battle CRUISERS &
Estimated about 500 Shells fired
91 Killed including 30 WOMEN & 15 CHILDREN
about 300 Wounded; Gasometer, Waterworks &
Towns much damaged

TYNEMOUTH
South Shields
SUNDERLAND

Docks
Seaton Carew
Shelled
Trees Mouth
Whitby to Hartlepool 28 Miles
REDCAR
SALTBURN
MIDDLESBROUGH

HELIGOLAND NAVAL BASE to HARTLEPOOL 330 Nautical Miles or about
14 HOURS PASSAGE for a FAST CRUISER SQUADRON at 22-25 Knots
their average speed; the
journey can therefore be
done under cover of NIGHT

WHITBY Bombarded 9.15 to about 9.30 a.m.
by 2 Battle CRUISERS, about 30
shells fired; 2 Men killed, 2 Boys
wounded; Coastguard Sta. ABBEY,
Town & inland villages damaged

St Hilda's Church
WHITBY
The ABBEY
Shelled
RUSWARP
Shelled
EAST
CLIFF
River ESK

Fylingdale Moor

ROBIN HOOD'S
BAY

RAVENSCAR

Petard Point

SCALBY

NORTH BAY
OLD CASTLE
Shelled.
OLD CASTLE WALL
Damaged
St MARY'S CHURCH
Hit
SHOP Set
on FIRE
EASTBOROUGH
OLD
HARBOUR
NEW HARBOUR
LIGHTHOUSE
Damaged
MANY HOUSES HIT in
this crowded quarter.
BALMORAL
HOTEL Hit
PROSPECT ROAD
HOUSES Hit
GLADSTONE ROAD
HANOVER Rd
BARWICK ST
HOUSE Hit
VICTORIA
HOUSES
Hit
WESTBOROUGH
CRESCENT
RAILWAY STA.
TOWN HALL
ROYAL HOTEL
Hit
CAFE Struck
SOUTH BAY
FALSGRAVE ROAD
GRAND HOTEL
Struck 3 times
RAMSDALE PARK
VALLEY
ROAD
St MARTINS
CH. Damaged

SCARBOROUGH
Bombarded from 8.5 to 8.25 a.m.
by Battle CRUISER & Armoured
CRUISER, estimated about 300
Shells fired; 17 KILLED including 8 WOMEN & 4 CHILDREN
about 100 Wounded

SOUTH CLIFF
Shelled
PRINCE of WALES Hotel Hit

E. MORRELL

139.   A map showing details of the bombardment of Whitby and the East Coast in 1914.

140. Another view of Whitby Abbey, this time seen from the churchyard. The print, which is dated 1776, shows the tower which fell in 1830, and the great west doorway which suffered at the hands of German battleships.

WHITBY ABBEY. — THE WESTERN GATEWAY
BEFORE & AFTER
THE GERMAN BOMBARDMENT. DEC: 16TH. 1914.

141. On 16 December 1914, the town was outraged by bombardment from the sea by German battleships, which damaged the abbey, wrecked the coastguard station and caused damage to many homes. The following pictures show the western abbey doorway before and after the attack.

142 & 143. These two photographs show just some of the destruction which was brought about by the bombardment in 1914. A shell hit property in Spital Bridge, whilst West Hill House suffered a similar fate.

THE WILLIES' WHITBY EXPLOIT AND THE RESULT.

144. Whitby Abbey appeared in this political cartoon during the First World War. The drawings refer to the surprise bombardment of Whitby and the abbey by German naval vessels.

145.   Following the end of the First World War this mighty German battleship was brought into the harbour to be scrapped. Although enormous, it was able to pass through the bridge to the upper harbour.

146.   The immensity of the German vessel, the *Danzig*, seen here in the upper harbour, can be judged against the houses of Church Street behind it.

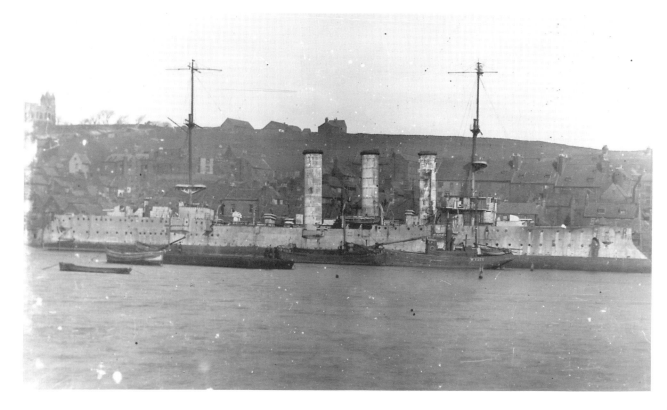

147.   This classic view of Whitby Abbey shows the monks' fish pond, which has shrunk somewhat over the years.

148. Captain James Cook's monument on Whitby's West Cliff. The statue, sculptured by Tweed, was unveiled on 16 July 1923 and was a gift from a former local M.P., Gervaise Beckett. A nearby weathervane featuring Cook's ship *Resolution* was given by Mrs. Cecil Broderick (of solicitors Bell, Broderick & Gray of London) replacing a copper dolphin on the same post.

149. This unusual picture of Captain Cook's ship *Discovery*, from the author's collection, is in sharp contrast to the official super-sleek images of the vessel portrayed on many official paintings. The ship is seen as it would have appeared shortly before its voyage to the South Seas.

150. The Iron Church, as it was commonly known, was actually called St Hilda's, and was hastily built to provide the residents of the newly-built West Cliff area with an alternate place of worship to the parish church on the other side of the river. It was later demolished, and replaced by the present St Hilda's, on the same site.

151. The church of St John the Evangelist is pictured here, shortly after it was built. The roadway has now been widened, and the high wall opposite has been demolished. Also vanished are the railings around the church, which no doubt were taken away for salvage during the Second World War.

LONDON HIBERNIAN SOCIETY.

On Thursday Evening, Sept. 27th, 1832,

THE REV. T. WEBSTER, M. A.,

VICAR OF OAKINGTON,

WILL PREACH A SERMON,

IN BAXTERGATE CHAPEL,

FOR THE BENEFIT OF THE

LONDON

HIBERNIAN SOCIETY,

For establishing Schools, and circulating the Holy Scriptures, in Ireland. Service to commence at half-past Six o'clock.

As the prospects of the Society are encouraging, and its Funds very low, it is hoped that the Collection will be liberal.

Whitby, Sept. 22nd, 1832.

152 & 153. The town has always been multi-denominational, and religious groups both great and small have been widely tolerated in the community. These two posters from 1832 show two local crusades.

IRISH EVANGELICAL SOCIETY.

On *SABBATH*, the 15th Inst.,

TWO SERMONS,

WILL BE PREACHED AT WHITBY,

BY THE REV. JOHN WILSON,

FROM IRELAND, FOR THE BENEFIT OF THE

IRISH

EVANGELICAL SOCIETY:

Viz. in the Morning, at half-past Ten, in *Silver-Street Chapel;* and at Two in the Afternoon, in *Cliff-Lane Chapel.*

The object of the Irish Evangelical Society is to promote the preaching of the Gospel in Ireland, as the most likely means for dispelling that moral darkness which has so long obscured and degraded this interesting part of the British empire.

A Collection will be made at each Service, and if any who cannot attend the Sermons, feel disposed to contribute towards the important object of this Society, their donations will be thankfully received by the Rev. George Young, A. M., or the Rev. William Blackburn.

Whitby, April 6th, 1832.

154. Long dresses and straw boaters evoke Edwardian days when John Bull reigned supreme, and Britannia ruled the waves. The scene is the town's West Cliff Saloon, later to become the Spa Floral Pavilion. It was recently redeveloped to provide facilities and entertainment which cater for more modern tastes.

155. Around 80 years ago, girls from St Michael's school, on Whitby's east side, took part in a concert at the Coliseum playhouse, now a cinema and bingo hall. The girls are pictured here at the time of the concert, together with three of their teachers. Only one of the group, Emma Hill (second from right, back row), is known.

56. Brass band competitions were a common form of entertainment in the district at the turn of the century. A photographer in 1907 captured this group who were all presumably North Eastern Railway employees. Unfortunately, apart from one band member, Walter Agar (3rd from right, middle row), the bandsmen's names are not recorded.

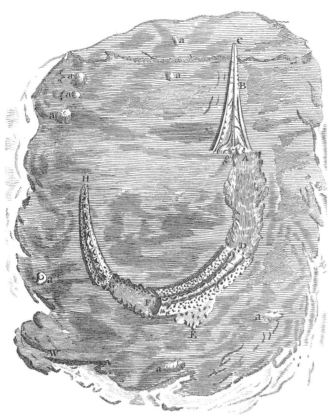

157.   In the 1700s the town became well-known to the scientific world when a number of large fossilised creatures were discovered in the cliffs. This engraving of 1758, made locally, depicts one of the first large fossils found in the area. Whitby museum still boasts one of the best collections of fossils in Britain.

158.   Lector Nab was a rocky outcrop on Whitby beach, from where this photograph was taken. It has long since been washed away by the action of the sea. The cliffs have now been stabilised and a sea wall runs along the base of the cliffs seen here.

159. Whitby's quaint and strange Penny Hedge, or Horngarth ceremony, which, it is said, has been performed continuously since the early days of Whitby Abbey. According to legend the small hedge must stand three tides or manor lands will be forfeited. This picture shows a Mr. Hutton, with mallet, whilst an assistant blows 'Out On Ye' three times.

160. A close-up of the hedge which is always built in the same manner, using a prescribed number of hazel sticks.

161. Another picture of the ceremony.

162. In the early days, before proper quays were constructed, it was common for collier cats (coal carrying ships with flat bottoms) to be run ashore on the beach in order to unload their cargo, or to take on provisions. This picture captures one such scene close to the west pier, as it looked before the building of extensions around 1910.

163.　Early days on the beach below the West Cliff. Holidaymakers were later provided with a Cliff Lift, still in use, which was reached by a tunnel at the bottom that connected with a shaft to the top. In recent years stabilisation work and new pathways have greatly altered the outline of the cliffs themselves.

164. Tuckers Field, on Whitby's West Cliff, is now associated with sports such as tennis, miniature golf, swimming, and a whole range of holiday pastimes. In the days when this photograph was taken it was still Tuckers Farm. It would appear that West Cliff school had not yet been built, though St Hilda's church can be seen in the background.

165. A once popular song which is still sung locally, and begins 'Barefoot days, when we were just a coupla kids ...', reminds many of the older generation of the days when times were hard, and many wore shoes only for best. These children (some without shoes), photographed whilst gathering firewood for their parents, are another reminder of such times.

166. Though rather gory to modern eyes, this scene would be commonplace to people at the turn of the century, who were used to seeing the slaughter of cows, pigs, etc., even at the back of butchers' shops. It is interesting to note that the children in the picture find the camera more curious than the killing about to take place.

167 & 168. Between the wars, local people would picnic at Saltwick tea-gardens. The area is now desolate, but once attracted hundreds of adults who would buy teas, sweets and lemonade whilst their children played on nearby swings, provided for patrons only. These two pictures show the thatched building and its grounds, shortly before it fell into decay.

169. Khyber Pass connecting Pier Road with the West Cliff area is seen here, along with the ridge of land known as Spion Kop. In recent years a dig was made in search of the cannon in the picture, but it was never found. It is now believed that it may have been sold for its scrap metal value.

170. The fog siren at Whitby High Light has gone forever. Its moaning cry in foggy weather could be heard throughout the district and way out to sea. Known locally as the Hawsker Bull or the Bawling Bull, it became redundant in 1988. A manual siren of *c.*1904, worked by bellows, preceded it.

171.   Though posted in 1910, this photograph was taken some time before this, as the pier extensions, completed in that year, are not in the scene. It shows the bandstand at the West Cliff Saloon. In later years a glass Spa Floral Pavilion was built over the area in the photograph, to be replaced by the present Spa complex.

172.   A final look back towards Whitby from the sea, with the abbey (and the site of the fog horn) to the left. The date is around 1860 and the cliff is shown as still connected to the east pier (without its modern extension). The sails of Union Mill can be seen above the then new West Cliff developments.